I Wish I Knew This 20 Years Ago...

Understanding the universal laws that govern all things

by Justin Perry

YouAreCreators.org

Check out our YouTube Channel, "YouAreCreators

YouAreCreators,Inc

Contents

Dedication

To my sons: Justin Jr, Joshua & Jaxon -- you bring me more joy than I can ever describe, and I am proud to see the brilliant creators you are becoming. To Ericka: my best friend, business partner, and Wife -- you are more than I can ever ask for in a spouse. I thank God everyday for the opportunity to look into those beautiful, almond shaped eyes. You are a piece of me. To my loving parents: who have been together for 30+ years -- you are the perfect example of love and companionship. To my older siblings: Duane, Tarin, Tai, and Kelli -- thank you for being there for me WHENEVER I needed you. I truly love you all!

Introduction

"Realize that now, in this moment of time, you are creating. You are creating your next moment based on what you are feeling and thinking. That is what's real."
— Doc Childre

Let me start off by saying, you've been lied to. Life is so much easier and simpler than you've been told. This writing is a collage of philosophical teachings and lessons that I have adopted through the years. I have tried and tested these teachings on myself, and they have worked for me every time without fail.

Several of these teachings might seem foreign to some of you and downright crazy to others, but believe me, they work and will always work. I have always been an inquisitive type of person, seeking knowledge wherever I could.

I question everything, and I need to know why things work the way they do. I finally found the answer to many of my questions while researching the universal laws that governs all things.

See, we are working with these universal laws, and just like the laws of gravity, the universal laws work and will always work. These laws have been talked about in every religion, sacred teaching, and scripture throughout history, yet few people know and understand them. Those who have obtained this knowledge have risen to enormous heights in their careers and personal endeavors.

This is my attempt to share this knowledge with you. So I decided to put together a short, to the point, no fluff, bullet point style manuscript of the teachings and philosophies that have changed my life, and continue to change the lives of countless others. This works without fail, if you would only try it for yourself.

Reality

"If we understood the power of our thoughts, we would guard them more closely. If we understood the awesome power of our words, we would prefer silence to almost anything negative..."
– Bettie Eadie

- We literally create our reality. This first bullet point is a brief synopsis of the entire book. To some, this may sound absurd and downright crazy, and to others it may sound accurate, but this statement is absolutely true. I would not be wasting my time writing this book if this concept was utter nonsense, but I am living proof. I would not have believed this if this simple truth had not proved itself over and over again.

- Throughout history, every wise man, philosophers, and holy man has come to the same conclusion: we become what we think about. But now, modern science (Quantum Physics) has come to the same conclusion. Quantum Physics now states that the mind is actually constructing and manipulating the physical world we live in.

- Quantum Mechanics states that everything is vibrating energy, and since everything is energy, everything has a frequency.

- In the spiritual world, like energy attracts like energy, so the frequency your energy is vibrating on is attracting other energy that is similar to that.

- A lot of what I'm about to tell you is still a mystery to us humans; we haven't discovered the mechanics behind why this "Thought" technology works. But after years of trial and error, tests and experiments, we have learned how to use this technology to bring about personal desires and outcomes.

- There are four major tools that are used when creating your reality; these tools are: Thoughts, Words, Feelings, and Actions. Each of these instruments produces a form of energy. Let's learn about these tools of creation and how we can use them to create whatever it is we desire in our lives.

On Tools of Creation: Thoughts and Words

"The thought manifests as the word. The word manifests as the deed. The deed develops into habit. And the habit hardens into character. So watch the thought and its ways with care. And let it spring from love, born out of concern for all beings."
– Buddha

- Be careful of the words you speak, for your words are extremely creative in the physical world.

- The Bible tells it like this, "Life and death is in the power of the tongue". This means, you can create a beautiful life with the words you speak or you can burn your life to the ground using the same instrument.

- Continuously speaking words of love, gratitude, and prosperity will eventually bring those things into your life.

- Words are thoughts that have been expressed, and those expressed thoughts, once spoken, get moved out into the universe as commands. Watch your words.
- Speak well of others, for what you say about them, will be said about you. This is a spiritual law.
- If we hold a positive thought and feeling, we attract positive situations, people, and objects that match that thought and feeling.
- If we are speaking negative words, we are attracting negative situations, people, and circumstances that match those words.
- Why not speak well of others and support them in their life situations? It will have to be returned to you in one form or another.
- Words are an extremely vibratory force in the universe.
- The vibrations of the spoken word affect the universe with greater impact. Greater than just mere thought.
- Watch what you say; you're always attracting the equivalent of your residual words.
- Talk about what you want as if you already have it.

- Play make-believe like a child and miracles will happen.
- This world we live in is a hologram projected from our residual thoughts and the frequencies of our emotional vibrations.
- Control the weather and escape the storm. (Metaphor)
- Let your words act as soldiers, bringing back to you all the good you've previously spoken.
- The world is at your command. (Literally)
- Every thought you think, and every word you speak is an affirmation.
- Don't entertain negative thoughts: The more you entertain negative thoughts, the more negative thoughts will enter your mind.
- Like will always attract like.
- When a negative thought enters your mind, and you entertain that thought with feeling and emotion, you are actually giving power to that thought. That is why it's important to nip negative thinking in the bud and quickly switch to a better feeling thought.

- Whenever a negative thought tries to enter your mind, don't give it any attention and consciously focus on something that brings you happiness. It can be a person or an object, anything that changes your mood and thinking.

- If you keep focused on positive things, sooner or later you will attract so many like-minded positive thoughts that you won't even remember the negative thought you were dwelling on.

- Talk about what you want: Society teaches us to complain about our problems and the things that are displeasing us at the moment. But all that does is perpetuate a negative cycle, thus bringing more things we don't want.

- Talk about the good things in life and about the prosperity and good health you are experiencing.

- Train your mind to only focus on the things you want to manifest in your life. You can do this by monitoring the feelings, thoughts and words you use most often.

- If there is a certain word or thought that you often use that doesn't serve you, get rid of it. Instead, talk about the lifestyle you prefer and about the good that is constantly flowing in your life. Let this be your dominate speech and thought pattern.

- The Law of Reaping and Sowing (cause and effect): What you give out is what you get back; you will always reap what you have sow.

- Whatever seed you plant in the soil of your mind, this will produce exactly after its kind.

- You have to reap what you have sown, whether it's positive or negative, failure or success.

Feelings and Actions for Abundance

"If constructive thoughts are planted, positive outcomes will be the result. Plant the seeds of failure and failure will follow."
– Sidney Madwed

- You are here to experience life the way you most desire. In the physical world you need wealth to do that. Therefore it is necessary to make friends with money on a mental level.

- Money is nothing but energy, and you can attract that energy into your life by feeling as though you ALREADY acquired it.

- I literally talk to my money. I tell it, "We are friends, I give you away, and you come back to me multiplied." After I do this, I get a feeling of wealth and assurance that comes over me, and when I hold that feeling, the universe somehow, always supplies me with more money.

- Go on a two week "news fast". The evening news spews hatred, destruction, and all forms of negativity. Subconsciously the message the broadcaster gives is clinging to you like a leach. Break free from the news and watch how your view of the world turns positive.

- The Law of Attraction: The Law of Attraction (my favorite universal law) states that like attracts like in the physical world. Everything is a form of energy, even your feelings. So whatever you are feeling this very moment is in the process of becoming a reality.

- Whatever frequency your feelings are vibrating on is an exact replica of your outside world.

- If you are feeling prosperous, life will keep showing examples of you being prosperous: you'll receive a check in the mail, you'll find money on the sidewalk; and that friend who owes you 20 bucks will all of a sudden call and pay up. That's how it works.

- We are all spiritually connected, and since we are connected, what I do to others has to come back around to me. This is universal law; this is the perfect justice.

- Don't be afraid to give away large portions of money. The universal Law of Reaping and Sowing or the Law of Attraction states that what you give has to be returned to you. But for some odd reason, it's usually multiplied!

- Smiling at a random stranger or simply saying "How you are doing?" is more powerful and important than you realize.

- A simple smile is a transference of positive energy to an individual, which causes a ripple effect. This random stranger will now send that positive energy to the next person, and so the cycle continues.

- One small act of kindness can change the world.

- Writing a list of your goals with a deadline is vastly important. How does a captain know where to go without an outlined map?

- Too many people are floating aimlessly with no clear direction in life.

- Here's a tip; if you don't know what your life's purpose

is, start writing down the things you love doing that somehow bring joy to other people.

- Your mission will always involve some form of service and it will always bring you an intense joy and fulfillment (i.e., a doctor, actor, business owner, or inventor).

- A wise man is always aware of his mood. For what he feels, he draws into his life.

- Your mood, or emotion is the architect of your life experiences.

- Train yourself to always be aware of how you're feeling. You can do this by forming a habit of constantly observing how you feel. It will be slightly difficult at first, but once it's second nature, you won't have to think about it.

- Just feel a little better. Don't try to take major leaps from feeling extremely negative to feeling extremely positive. Just feel a little better. That little positive energy will attract other energy that is positive, and once you create momentum the snowball effect is produced, and you will be right as rain.

- To master creating your reality, you have to be aware of what you're feeling at any moment. You monitor this by reminiscing the feelings that created a particular reality. How did you feel? Did you dwell on it or was it just a passing thought? If you can remember the feeling of your last creation, you can create anything using that same emotional frequency. Find the feeling.

- You will become what you act like: There is a term, "fake it, till you make it". Some people look down on this strategy, but I absolutely love it. This is exactly what I did when I started YouAreCreators. I told myself everyday that "I have the largest self-help YouTube channel in the world!", and "I am a world famous motivator!" I said this enough times that I actually started to believe it, even when there wasn't a sign in sight. I acted as if it was already true and that is when things actually became true. Life started bringing me all the things necessary to make those dreams true: I got emails from people offering advice and authors contacted me and asked if I could post some of their material. Everything fell in place to make my affirmation a reality.

- Remember the feeling: When I was younger, I remember every so often, a feeling would come over me and I would be able to make 90% of the shots I would take in a basketball game. It was as if the basketball hoop was the size of a barrel; I simply couldn't miss. Many basketball players call this state of mind "being in the zone". It's as if the super-conscious mind completely takes over and you are a super version of you. I have also found that many famous basketball players could turn this "zone" on at will, and they did this by remembering the feelings they had while they were in the zone the last time.

- This "zone" can be applied towards anything you can think of, such as business, school work, invention ideas, and even social events.
- We all have this ability to tap into the super-conscious mind, and we can do this by rekindling the feelings of how we felt before.
- Remember, feelings and emotions are the driving force of creation. Whatever we put intense feelings behind manifest quickly in our reality.
- If you can match the feelings or the mood that you held during any past situation, you will produce the same outcome, guaranteed.

How to Be Your Best and Expect the Best

"You get what you expect in life. Expect great things in life. Live your best life."
– Lailah Gifty Akita

- The average human lifespan is 84 years (that's being generous), so why would you settle for anything that is less than best? I mean the best of EVERYTHING!

- Most people don't want to have the best because they feel it's too expensive and they can't afford it. For example, if you're buying a blender, and they have two versions, the Blender S1 or the Blender S1 Deluxe, get the Blender S1 Deluxe! You deserve it, and there is always enough money. The universe/God is unlimited and will support ANY financial belief you create for yourself.

- God/universe is supporting you at EVERY turn and in ALL subjects.
- Whatever you truly believe, God/universe is moving mountains and obstacles to match your belief! Positive or negative... so focus on the positive.
- If you believe you aren't good enough, the universe will match that belief and prove you right.
- If you believe that you deserve the best out of life, that universe will prove you right. So what do you believe?
- Type up a list of about 6 positive affirmations and put them in places you can spot them in the morning. Make sure these are affirmations and are phrases that you can accept. You can tell if you accept them by the way they make you feel.
- Say these affirmations out loud and with strong conviction. You might look crazy, but who cares! Your life is changing!

On Abundance

"Thought is the original source of all wealth, all success, all material gain, all great discoveries and inventions, and all achievement."
– Claude M. Bristol

- There is no such thing as lack. Screw what the evening news tells you!

- We live in a very abundant world that is always replenishing itself. If you don't believe me, look at the grass in your yard; there are more blades of grass than you can ever count. Or look at a fruit trees; there is more fruit that you can ever eat. So there is always enough, and when you believe that, it will always prove itself right.

- Focus on prosperity, and it becomes your reality.

- Reaping and Sowing is another name of a universal law. This universal law is always in effect and applies to every aspect of your life. Your thoughts, words, and actions are seeds that will produce after their own kind. If you plant poverty thoughts, and lack, that is what will produce. Plant thoughts of love, good health, prosperity, and harmony, and in due season, your garden will flourish in abundance.

- We live in an infinite universe; nature knows no lack.
- We are unlimited beings and we will always be unlimited beings.
- Whatever you imagine in your mind can be created in the physical world.
- There is no amount of money you can't have; there is no amount of joy you can't attain.
- Nothing is withheld from us, nothing!
- There is no shortage of anything, because the universe always regenerates itself.

- If it looks like supplies are dwindling, don't fret, more of the alternative will be produced.
- We are always provided, whether we realize it or not, but the thing is, when fear and doubt creep in, you can actually hinder those blessings from materializing.
- Remember, the universe organizes itself according to our beliefs, so if we believe that there is not enough, there won't be.
- If we believe we are provided for and there is plenty, there will be plenty. But you have to actually believe that. You have to train your mind to push past the fear and demand what you expect to be true.
- Abundance is all around you. If you need some examples, just look outside at the grass and the leaves on the trees. Nature always creates more than enough.

On How You Want Your Life to Be

By choosing your thoughts, and by selecting which emotional
currents you will release
and which you will reinforce, you determine the quality of
your life.
You determine the effects that you will have upon others, and
the nature of the
experiences of your life.

– Gary Zukav

- Play make-believe. Write a script about how you would like your life to be, from how much money you want, to your dream career, and the house you would like to live in.
- Now close your eyes and live the experience, smell the smells, say the words, drive that car, live in that home.

- Make a vision board: Buy some poster paper, and cut and paste the people, objects and goals you desire most. Look at it every day, and FEEL as if you already have it!

- If you hold that vision and perform that every day, the universe seeks to match that creation.

- These are powerful tools in creating the life that you want; this is visualizing in its highest form.

The Power Of The Mind

"Eventually it became clear that our emotions, attitudes, and thoughts profoundly affect our bodies, sometimes to the degree of life or death. Soon mind-body effects were recognized to have positive as well as negative impacts on the body. This realization came largely from research on the placebo effect—the beneficial results of suggestion, expectation, and positive thinking."
– Larry Dossey

- Your thoughts, words, and emotions are extremely powerful. So much that scientists now believe that humans literally affect the world around them (i.e., plants, the weather, water, etc.).

- When you have a group of people that thinks the same way, with the same intention, there will be manifestation on a LARGE scale, whether positive or negative. In 1993, a group of scientist (led by Dr. John Hagelin) in Washington, DC conducted an experiment in which a number of 4,000 people would meditate on peace, twice a day for two months. The results were quite impressive with a 24.6% decrease in violent crimes. There has also been experiments that suggest that a collective amount of people can even affect the weather!

- The Placebo Effect is a well known experiment, proving the power of the mind. Scientist preformed a experiment of 20 patients with severe food allergies. They gave 10 patients allergy medication, and gave the other 10 patients only sugar pills, but told the patients it was the highly advanced allergy medication. The results were startling! They found that both set of patients scored the exact same, a 75% success rate of getting rid of the food allergy.

- Princeton students conducted an experiment where they hosted a party and told everyone that there was free beer in the kegs. What they didn't tell them, was the kegs were filled with non alcoholic beer. The students that drank the beer thought they were drinking transitional beer, thus believing they were getting drunk. The end result were, students passed out on the lawn, stumbling in the street, and slurring their words, simply by BELIEVING they were drunk.

- Physicists have even concluded that their expectations somehow affect the experiments they are conducting.

- If you train your mind to only expect positive situations, positive outcomes, and positive events, the world around you will transform, and your dominate life experiences will yield to your expectations.

On Changing Your Frequency/Mood

"The greatest discovery of any generation is that a human can alter his life by altering his attitude."
– William James

- Quantum Physicists have now concluded that our world consists of multiple frequencies of vibrations including your thoughts.

- Based on the universal Law of Attraction, "Like attracts Like". So if you're in a "feel GOOD" frequency, you will attract people, circumstances, and situations to match that "feel GOOD" frequency. If you're in a "feel BAD" frequency, you will continue to attract people, circumstances, and situations that will match that frequency and continue to feel bad.

- Change to a good feeling frequency and watch how your world transforms into a big, positive melting pot.

On the View of Multiple Dimensions and Parallel Realities

"Everything is energy and that's all there is to it. Match the frequency of the reality you want and you cannot help but get that reality. It can be no other way. This is not philosophy. This is physics."

– Darryl Anka

- Everything you want is already in existence.

- Quantum Physics has come to the conclusion (String Theory) that there are multiple dimensions and parallel realities.

- Each parallel reality has a version of you in it, doing any and every situation you can think of. There's a version of you being a homeless person, there's also a version of you being the wealthiest person in the city.

- Based on where your attention goes and based on the actions you take, there is no limit to who you can become.
- In a sense, you already have the things you desire, you simply aren't experiencing themyet.
- If you focus on lack, you will shift into that reality.
- If you focus on abundance and success, you will vibrate at the same frequency, thus propelling you move into that reality. This is simple physics.

On Meditation

"To understand the immeasurable, the mind must be extraordinarily quiet, still."
– Jiddu Krishnamurti

- If you're feeling stressed out, overwhelmed, or simply can't get your thoughts together, find a quiet place and meditate.

- Meditation has many wonderful benefits, such as: calmness, relaxation, and emotional balance. It also increases immunity, sharpens creativity, improves your mood, and helps to develop intuition.

- All these benefits will help you live a more balanced, relaxed life.

- When feeling stressed out, do a 15 second mediation. Instructions: breathe in through your nose for 5 seconds, hold your breath for 5 seconds, and then exhale through your nose for 5 seconds; all the while thinking to yourself, "All is well" over and over again.

This simple mediation will bring you instant serenity and peace.

- When you feel overwhelmed, spend time in solitude and get back in "the flow". As actor Hugh Jackson describes, "Bathing in the creative energy that permeates all things." This can also be called meditation. Get back to peace.

- If you slow down your mind with meditation, the world will follow suit. Life is nothing but a mirror reflecting back to you of what you project first. If you're hectic, your world will be hectic; if you're harmonious, your world will be in harmony.

On Self-Affirmations

"The man who succeeds must always in mind or imagination live, move, think, and act as if he had gained that success, or he never will gain it."

– Prentice Mulford

- Affirmations are one of the most powerful tools you can have in your creative tool box.

- Affirmations should always be done in the present tense. "I am" or "I Have"

- The most powerful statement you will ever use with your affirmations is "I-Am".

- Those two words (I-Am) are the greatest creative force that will ever come out of your mouth: I-Am Happy, I-Am wonderful, I-Am Healthy, I-Am Wealthy, I-Am abundant, I-Am- Prosperous.

- When doing affirmations, make sure that you are putting feelings and emotions behind them.

- I often close my eyes and yell my affirmations in the

shower; that way I can feel what I'm saying and confidence seems to be imbedded in the words.

- Try it, you'll feel a rush of energy afterward.
- Don't be afraid to speak out loud to yourself.
- Self affirmations are a vital tool in creating your reality and the desires you want to experience.
- When I'm feeling or thinking negatively, I often counter with some positive verbal command that often starts with "I am". Such as "I am creative", "I am positive", "I am strong". These verbal commands make me feel strong, and therefore, I am strong.
- The two most powerful words in the universe, I-AM: These two words are so powerful that inancient times, it was forbidden to use them and this was even punishable by death.
- The words "I-Am" are believed by many to be the name God gave to Moses.
- These two words "I-AM" encompasses all of life and the universe combined.
- When we invoke these words, we are announcing the

presence of God within us.

- Whatever we put behind those two words is created in astounding time and accuracy.

- Therefore, it is important to monitor what we attach to those words. I often hear people saying things like, "I-am Broke", "I-am sick". These statements will continue to produce similar states of being.

- When I learned of this truth, I completely changed my vocabulary. My personal "I-Am's" are "I -am Healthy"," I am prosperous", I am wise", and "I am generous".

- Speak these with conviction and authority! Say them until you actually start to believe them; that's when the magic starts!

On Giving

"Love only grows by sharing. You can only have more for yourself by giving it away to others."
– Brian Tracy

- The act of giving is always the cornerstone for abundance.

- Most people believe when you give something away, you actually lose it; but that couldn't be further from the truth. When you give, it seems like the universe is pleased with that action and in return, you're blessed with more.

- Giving is such a natural act that after you do it, you get a rush of endorphins and other good feeling natural chemicals that flood the body.

- If you give what you have, you will never go without.

- Law of Reaping and Sowing, if you give, you have to receive. There is no way around it. So why not share what you have? This is a sure way of always having enough, and also, it feels so darn good!

- When you horde what you have (in fear that there won't be enough), that energy has a way of self-destructing and you eventually end up losing everything.

- Remember, you attract what you love, but you also attract what you fear.

- When you fear losing money or property, you charge those possibilities with emotion, and emotion is the force that attracts!

- Fear not and give what you can... life will be good!

On Trusting the Process

"Trust that out of every situation, good will come. When you choose to believe that good will come out of every experience, you'll soon discover that perceived obstacles are really blessings in disguise."

– Denise Marek

- When you write down your desires and walk toward your goals, trust that everything that happens to you is for your good and is actually leading you to accomplish your goals.

- The universe works in ways we don't and can't understand; but when the smoke clears and the dust settles, we will notice that every step we took aided our success.

- Enjoy the ride.
- Trust your feelings.
- If it doesn't feel right, it probably isn't: universal intelligence (God) is always communicating with you, and it's through your feelings.
- If you want to see if something is right or not, see how you feel about it.
- It's as if your feelings go into the future and recognize if the situation is good or bad for you.
- Trust your gut.

On Challenging Times

"In times of great stress or adversity, it's always best to keep busy, to plow your anger and your energy into something positive."
– Lee Iacocca

- Build a tough skin, you're built for this world.
- Just because you're positive, doesn't mean you won't have challenging times.
- We need challenging times to build our character and further our spiritual growth.
- Don't run from your trials but face them head on.
- If you resist, your trials will persist. Face them head on and command your reality.
- Be strong and face that giant on your pathway.
- There is a lesson and opportunity in challenging times, seize the moment!

On Guidance

"You need to trust, to surrender.
To ask for guidance , go within for the answers.
They're within you, you have the answers. All you need do is ask"
– Karen Hackel

- You are never alone.

- We all have angels or spirit guides that are always with us.

- They will help you if you ask them; it's that simple.

- It is their greatest pleasure assisting us with life's endeavors.

- Trust your gut or intuition (one of their avenues of communication); they are always talking and assisting us.

- If something happens you don't particularly like or expect, bless it and expect a positive outcome.

- You won't understand everything now, but when its all

said and done, you'll see that you have been guided toward your life's mission.

- Listen to your intuitive guides.
- It has been said that each person has been given two or more personal angels or spirit guides.
- When you come to a fork in the road, seek assistance and they will be more than happy to assist you.
- Watch for clues: the next song you hear over the radio, the sign you read while you're driving, or the conversation you overhear, God uses all these to assist you.
- Trust your gut, that little voice inside you. That is the voice of God. It will never steer you wrong and will guide you toward your highest good.

- I can recall a number of times where I was indecisive on which route to take, but after a few minutes of quiet meditation I received guidance in the form of inspired action. Trust those moments.

- Sometimes you need to get out of your own way, and let your angels guide you to your happiness.

- When you are stuck at a crossroad, sit in meditation, and ask your angels to help you.

- You are surrounded by angels that will help you, if you ask them for help. But you have to ask.

- After you ask, watch for leads, trust your gut, and walk in positive expectancy.

On the Meaning of Numbers (Signs from Angels) and the Power of Numbers

"God is a Mathematician"
– Mario Livio

- When we see a set of numbers over and over throughout the day, that is a sign from your angels to listen.

- For example, one day I kept seeing the number "222". I saw this number at least 3 times in 3 different places, so I decided to investigate. I Googled, "numbers keep appearing" and what I found shocked and comforted me. I found that when you keep seeing the same sequence of numbers, those are your angels communicating with you. They are often called "angel numbers".

- It helped me because at the time, I was going through a

period of uncertainty and doubt, and "222" means that all is well, everything is going to be alright, and the situation is working out better than you expected.

- That was exactly what I needed to hear and my angels have never let me down.

- Here are some other angel numbers that might show in your life: "111"- means to make sure you are focused on what you want instead of what you don't want. This is a period in time where the universe is rapidly manifesting your thoughts. If what you are thinking is negative, change those thoughts to positive now!

- (Since we already did "222", I'll go straight to "333".)

- "333"- means that "...the ascended masters such as Jesus, Buddha, St. Christopher, Muhammad, Quan Yin, whoever you are spiritually connected to, are nearby and are ready to assist you in your struggle or difficulty." All you have to do is ask.

- "444"- means that you are surrounded by a slew of angels who love and support you. Your connection to the spirit world is strong and they stand ready to assist you; all is well.

- "555"- means get ready, because something is about to change in your life. This change can be what you have been asking for or it could be simply a part of your soul's journey. If you call the situation positive, it will be positive. If you call the situation negative, it will be negative. But the situation is neutral in itself.

- "666"- means you are temporarily out of alignment with Source (God). Your thoughts are not in harmony with the positive flow of life, and if you persist in that negative thinking frequency, negative will manifest in your life. Change your thoughts and feelings!

- "777"- means the spirit world is celebrating the wonderful service you are offering your fellow man. Keep up the good work, for you are operating in your life's purpose and mission. This is an extremely positive sign, letting you know you are on the right track.

- "888"- means that financial abundance is on its way, and it will arrive to you at the perfect time. You are now reaping the financial abundance that you have sown from your past thoughts, words, feelings, and actions. "888" could also mean that a phase in your life is ending (i.e., a career or broken relationship). But don't fret, it's turning out better that you expected.

- "875" - means that the track you're on will lead you to material wealth and abundance. Stay on this path and prosperity will be yours in common hours.

- "999" - means you should be doing more to make the world a better place; you're here to be a light into the world, not to be stationary. Get up and start acting on your life's mission as the world needs what you have.

- "000" - means it is a sign, reminding you of how powerful you truly are and how you are connected to GOD. You are an unlimited being with the ability to manifest anything you want on this planet, remember that.

- "123" is telling you to discard of anything that doesn't serve you in your life. If it's negative and drains you of your positive energy, leave it alone. If it doesn't nourish your soul, get rid of it.

On Creativity

"Nobody works better under pressure. They just work faster."
– Brian Tracy

- Don't think too much. We can over-think our way out of a good thing.

- When reaching for our goals, we have a tendency to over think and over-analyze situations.

- One of the keys we have to remember is creativity cannot be forced.

- Creativity comes from a relaxed, chilled out mind.

- We have to trust God and get our human (conscious) mind out of the equation.

- The universe knows more than you, and it can deliver you an answer to the equation you're dealing with.

- Let your super-conscious mind (i.e. the mind where all the brilliant ideas flow) take over and watch miracles happen.

- Don't think, don't try, just do!

On Reading, Audiobooks, Snippets of Motivation, and Healing Frequencies

"I cannot remember the books I've read any more than the meals I have eaten; even so, they have made me."
– Ralph Waldo Emerson

- What are you reading? What you read, pours heavily on your subconscious mind.

- Make sure what you're reading is constructive and leading toward your goals.

- If you want to be a leader, read books on leadership.

- If your goal is to be a CEO of a company, read biographies of successful CEOs.

- Whatever you feed your mind, produces in the physical world.

- Throughout the day, play audiobooks and snippets of motivation. Your conscious mind may not always hear it, but your subconscious mind is always picking it up.

- Think of your subconscious mind as your own personal secretary, always picking up what you say and hear.

- If the subconscious mind hears something long enough and enough times, it starts to recognize it as truth, thus forming new beliefs.

- It would benefit you greatly to impress the subconscious with messages of success, prosperity, and positive thinking patterns.

- What you feed your mind is what you'll get in life.

- Certain frequencies produce certain effects in the body. One of those frequencies is 528hz.

- 528hz has been used for centuries by monks and other spiritual gurus to fight off illness and restore the body. Many people believe that it can even heal damaged DNA.

- Nature celebrates 528hz and all of life resonates with it.
- 528hz has been used to purify and separate oil from water during ocean oil spills.
- I would highly recommend meditation to this powerful audio (download it for free at YouAreCreators.org) or even play it on repeat while you sleep. My wife and I use this and we haven't experienced the common cold in quite a while!
- You'll wake up refreshed and recharged.

On Moderation

"An over-indulgence of anything, even something as pure as water, can intoxicate."
– Criss Jami

- Everything in moderation. Too much of anything will cause a burden in your life. Balance is the name of the game.
- It's vital that you take time off to recharge your batteries, even time off doing the things you love.
- When you come back, you'll have more energy and a plethora of new ideas.
- Even Jesus spent 40 days alone in a desert.

On Being Child-like

"Every child is an artist. The problem is how to remain an artist once he grows up."
– Pablo Picasso

- Be as little children, have child-like faith and imagination.

- When we were kids, our main objective was to be happy. Any and everything made us laugh and we found joy in the smallest things. But when we got older, we lost that sense of being and replaced it with fear.

- I maintain my child-like mind by taking the worry-free approach to life. I have successfully ingrained in my subconscious mind that whatever happens is ultimately for my good. And since I believe this, it is. I also keep my playful side open by watching funny movies and laughing until my side hurts.

- Go run in the snow, have a water gun fight outside, dance in the rain.

- It's the little immature things that keep life a picnic.

- Stop keeping it real: In my generation, there was a phrase that I heard quite often, it was "keep it real". That phrase is one of the most growth stunting, perpetuating statements one can make. Keeping it real will keep you exactly where you are now, blurring your vision for the future. It's basically telling you to think logically, and stop using your imagination. If everyone thought logically, there would be no airplanes, cell phones, or radio broadcasts.

- Stop thinking logically; logical thinking produces logical results.

- Successful men and women don't think logically; they believe in the things that seem improbable to the average person. And since they believe in the improbable, they produce those results in their world.

- If someone tells you to "keep it real", remember, you create what's real.

On Creating Happiness

"Folks are usually about as happy as they make their minds up
to be."

– Abraham Lincoln

- Don't look for happiness, create it.

- Life should be a constant unfolding of joy.

- If we are unhappy or in a low mood, we have only
  temporarily forgotten our connection to Source.

- Happiness is our natural state of being. That's why it
  feels good when you're happy, and miserable when
  you're not.

- We can get back into our natural state of being (Happy)
  by focusing on the things we're grateful for.

- Gratitude keeps us connected to God and reminds us
  how truly blessed we are.

- Write down on a sheet of paper all the things you're
  grateful for (IE, your health, the bones in your feet) you
  will automatically start to improve your mood.

On Personal Experience

"He knows the water best who has waded through it."
– Danish Proverb

- The best experience is personal experience.
- It's OK to take others' words on a subject, but it's better when you experience it yourself.
- Anything you read from this book, I recommend you try it for yourself. That is the only way for you to prove to yourself that this works.
- Either try it or deny it.
- Experience is the mother of learning.

On Being Connected and Divine Order

"I knew everything happened for a reason. I just wished the reason would hurry up and make itself known."
– Christina Lauren

- We are all one.
- What I do to someone, I literally do to myself.
- We're all connected in this quantum web.
- Quantum Physics has now confirmed that we are all connected on a quantum level.
- Physicists have performed a series of tests that prove what we now know as Quantum Entanglement.
- Physicists noticed when two particles interacted with each other, what is done to one particle has an immediate effect on the other, even if they are millions of miles away. In short, proving the fact that the universe is one big knitted grid, connecting all things.

- There's no such thing as coincidence in this world.

- God's universe is not random and nothing is wasted.

- When you start to evolve in consciousness, you will start to notice that your life is connected to everyone else in one small variation or another.

- Before we incarnated on this earth, we agreed to certain trials and opportunities to enhance our spiritual growth.

- Everything has a purpose and that purpose is ultimately for your highest good.

- When you recognize and acknowledge this, you're well on your way to your next positive adventure.

On Near-Death Experiences

"Humans are powerful spiritual beings meant to create good on the Earth. This good isn't usually accomplished in bold actions, but in singular acts of kindness between people. It's the little things that count, because they are more spontaneous and show who you truly are."

– Dannion Brinkley

- Based on the thousands of near-death experience cases I have read, and personally interviewed, they all have one thing in common: they all experience having a life review.

- A life review is either conducted by a guardian angel, family member, or a religious figure from your belief system.

- During that life review, they say that we will feel every emotion of every person we've ever affected. Even the feelings of the people we've affected that affected other people.

- Everything has a ripple effect.
- Every thought, word and intention send reverberations out in the universe. These reverberations even affect the people and the energy around you. The people that you have affected, now affect other people and so the ripple effect continues. Here's the kicker, what you put out has to come back to you, for that is the Law of Reaping and Sowing. Why not put out love, appreciation, and compassion?
- One act of kindness can spread around the world.
- I don't know about you, but I would like to see and feel all the people that I have affected on a positive level, rather on a negative level.
- I want my life review to a thing of beauty.
- So I'm challenging you to make your life review glorious and loving, up to this point.
- Each soul asked and volunteered to come to Earth.
- Thought Creates reality.
- Certain events are planned before birth, to carry out a purpose and hasten spiritual development.

- Your soul is eternal and cannot die.
- In the beginning every soul was with the creator.
- Your soul is literally a piece of God, we are extensions of the source.
- In the spirit world, your thoughts and emotions are manifested instantaneously.
- The purpose of life is spiritual growth and creation.
- You grow spiritually through love.
- God does not punish. Life is a series of cause and effects and reaping and sowing. When something happens to us we don't like, it isn't God punishing us, its a universal law that has taken place. We are always reaping what we have sown in one form or another.

On Financial Security

"You have a divine right to abundance, and if you are anything less than a millionaire, you haven't had your fair share."

– Stuart Wilde

- When you are financially secure, you now have the time to do what's really important.
- In the society we live in, money is essential to everyday life.
- Money is not the most important thing, but it is right up there with water. In Western culture, money is essential to living everyday life.
- The one thing that money can give you is your time. Your time is one of the most precious jewels we have.
- When you are financially secure, you can wake up and eat on your own schedule, and that's a beautiful thing.
- Money is vital to exploring God's creation and collecting life's experiences.

- Since money is energy, it has its own vibrational frequency. To vibrate with money, you must feel as if you have already acquired a large sum of it. Envision holding the money, smell it, say, "Thank you for my large sum of money."

- You'll hear a lot of millionaires say that "wealth is a feeling, it's a mindset"; and that is because it is.

- Millionaires, at their core beliefs, hold a strong conviction that there is only wealth. They don't talk about poverty; they don't think about poverty.

- If you want to join this club of prosperity, you must eliminate all thoughts and words that contradict this prosperous lifestyle.

- Never say, "I'm broke" or "I don't have any money". Those are commands to the universe. Instead, play make-believe and envision everyday living a prosperous life.

- When I first started conditioning my wealth, my mindset, I would sleep with money affirmations playing on repeat all night. I would adjust the volume just loud enough for me to hear it. After doing this for one year straight, I could totally see how my beliefs about money changed for the better.

- If you claim to be prosperous but only buy generic food for fear of "what if there isn't enough, let me save money", then that is an affirmation to the universe, telling it, "I don't have enough". And guess what... You won't.

- When you spend money, spend it fearlessly knowing that the universe is infinite and will always provide.

- Those who criticize money will always produce a lack of it.

- Ever notice that the people who always speak badly about money are usually struggling financially? It seems that they are always broke and never seem to make ends meet. That is because they have built negative belief patterns regarding money, thus causing their subconscious mind to self-sabotage any plans towards attaining money.

- Remember, if you have negative beliefs about money,

you will reap negative situations regarding money.

- If you want to attract more money in your life, you have to form a positive relationship with money.

- Think of money as a friend, a friend that gives you freedom to explore God's wonderful creation.

- Wealth is a byproduct of service: If you strive to make money just for the sake of making money, you'll end up hating what you're doing in the long run. The only way to prevent that is to create a service that you love and that provides some type of service that benefits others. The upside to that is you'll get paid for helping other people and you'll also get paid for doing what you love.

- These major companies that you see making untold millions and billions, all started with someone wanting to provide service to others in one way or another. The crazy thing about that is, the universe seems to jump on board with you and help you help other people.

- Have faith that every step will be provided for you along the way, and before you know it, you have a successful business.

- Here's the secret to prosperity; the more you share, the more you have to share. It's the boomerang effect.

- Giving has the opposite reaction of receiving, and by giving you are opening up the pathway for you to receive more.

- Those who give what they have, will never go without.

- A word of advice: when you give, your mood should be simply for the act and intention ofgiving; if your intention is pure, the universe will bless you in abundance.

On Taking Action on Your Dreams

"Follow your bliss and the Universe will open doors where there were walls."
– Joseph Campbell

- Take action on your dreams every day.
- The quote "faith without works is dead" is 100% true.
- You can visualize and speak things into existence all you want, but action is also a major part of the creation process.
- Not just any action, inspired action!
- We all have angels around us at all times, and these angels are constantly giving us clues and leads to accomplish our life mission. Our angels are the "Gut feeling" we often get.
- When you have a hunch to go some way or do something, do it! It could lead you to accomplishing

your goal.

- When working on your goals, the universe will give you leads of inspiration. Take those leads! You will know these leads because they will feel like joyous action instead of forced struggle.

- Remember the universe doesn't strain to do anything, not even showing you which direction to take.

- Whatever you look for, you're going to find: The Biblical scripture, "Seek and ye shall find" is truth down to the single word.

- Whatever you focus on is expanding in your reality, success or failure.

- If you notice, the things you put the most emphasis on keep showing up in your life.

- There's an old saying, "What you are seeking is also seeking you".

- Seek out/ focus on good health, abundance, prosperity, and peaceful surroundings, and you'll make them a dominant part of our life.

On Finding Your Passion

"Let yourself be silently drawn by the strange pull of what you really love. It will not lead you astray."
– Rumi

- The things you love to do, your passions, are not just some random feelings you have; they are your assignments.

- After reading book after book and hours of personal interviews, it has been revealed to me, that, before we incarnated in this world, we all agreed to accomplish certain goals that would hasten our spiritual evolution and the evolution of others.

- These goals are recognized as our passions, the thing or things we love doing that bring us the most joy.

- With our human understanding, we might perceive this goal to be small or big, but in the greater scheme of things, it's all part of the Divine plan. It's perfect.

- The wonderful thing is that our assignments bring us

the most happiness and fulfillment in life.

- Follow your bliss, you'll be happy you did.
- The desires and passions we have are not random but were given to us on a soul level.
- Our grandest desires are not just things we are passionate about; they are the assignments we have agreed to, before birth.
- God loves us so much that God made the things we absolutely love doing the main purpose for our existence.
- Most people think they can't make a living doing what they love doing, but that's only because they're entertaining negative, limiting thinking patterns. Anything is possible.

- Just because you don't know how you can do something, doesn't mean it can't be done.
- We must understand that our limited human thinking can only go so far (when we are negative), and infinite intelligence (God) knows the easiest and quickest way to bring your desires to you.
- Remember, the universe wants you to win.
- Everything is for you; nothing is against you, even if it seems like it is.
- All things work out for your good and you will recognize that when it's over.

On Raising Your Energy Level

"The higher your energy level, the more efficient your body. The more efficient your body, the better you feel and the more you will use your talent to produce outstanding results."

– Anthony Robbins

- Raise your energy so high that people cannot affect you.

- When I say raise your energy, I'm saying, raise that intense feeling of love that dwells within you so high, that negativity bounces off of you, like a ball bounces off concrete.

- There are a couple of things that can help raise your energy: meditation, expressing gratitude and love, dwelling on positive thoughts, and the ultimate… which is combining all 5.

- When you can combine these 5 tools, you will be able to control and manipulate the situations and circumstances that arise in your life.

- All energy is contagious: Ever notice how some people can walk in a room full of people and change the atmosphere? Well, we all have that power.
- When we feel extremely happy or extremely negative, that energy will topple the energy of those around us, thus merging our energy into theirs.
- You can make the atmosphere positive, or you can make it negative, and it all lies with the vibration/mood/attitude you hold.
- I would recommend choosing a mate that is known to have a positive vibration.
- If you have two negative people living in a household, only "negative" will be the result.
- When one person is positive, and the other is sometimes negative, the positive will always trump the negative.
- When you have two positive people living under one household... BOOM!
- Do yourself a favor, find a positive spouse. You two will be unstoppable!
- The greatest suppressed secret of man is that he is a part

of God (Source energy) and God is a part of him.

- Under any powerful microscope, you will see that you and everything else are made up of tiny packets of vibrating energy.
- Energy cannot be destroyed, or created, only converted from one form to another.
- All energy has to come from a source; this "Source" is what we refer to as God.
- God is the prime Creator, and we are extensions of that.

On Goal-Setting

"Our plans miscarry because they have no aim. When a man does not know what harbor he is making for, no wind is the right wind."
– Seneca

- Writing our goals is one of the most important tools in creating the reality you desire.

- Without goals, you're like a blindfolded archer; you're aiming everywhere.

- Goals are akin to a laser, a concentrated beam of light that aims and hits its target.

- Write your goals in crystal clear terms. Down to the color of the car, even the amount of rooms you want. Make sure that is clear and precise. If your goals are vague, you get vague results!

- Write your goals in the present tense, "I have" or "I am".

- Quantum Physics tells us that by simply focusing on

something literally brings it into solid form reality.

- We must focus on what we desire in order to manifest it in our lives.

- How can we manifest things in our lives if we don't have any set goals written down?

- I usually write down my annual goals at the beginning of January every year. All goals might not manifest in that year, but I guarantee if you hold true to them, they have to manifest for that is the law.

On Laughter

"I love people who make me laugh. I honestly think it's the thing I like most, to laugh. It cures a multitude of ills. It's probably the most important thing in a person."

– Audrey Hepburn

- One of the greatest metaphysical healing properties is laughter.
- Laughter raises the vibrations in the body and boosts the immune system while relieving stress.
- Dr. Len Horowitz talks about how the "HAHA" in laughter resonates with 528hz, which is known as the "Healing Frequency".
- The energy in laughter is so powerful that people have even demonstrated bending spoons after an intense laughing session.

- There are even multiple reports of patients ridding themselves completely of cancer using nothing but laughter by watching funny movies.
- Anytime you are "under the weather", watch a funny movie or be around someone you find hilarious. That is a guaranteed way to raise your energy and heal your body at the same time.

On Forming Habits

"A nail is driven out by another nail; habit is overcome by habit."
– Desiderius Erasmus

- It takes 21 to 30 days to form a complete habit. This information is powerful, because this allows you to take charge of your life and form new positive habits.

- I challenge you for 30 days, to listen to only positive audiobooks in your car or on your mp3 player. Play audiobooks and motivational seminars all day. While you sleep, put on positive affirmations and let them play throughout the night to impress the subconscious mind. During this time, also go on a "news fast". This means you can't watch the daily news or listen to the news at all.

- Watching the news has a funny way of bringing down your vibration and making you feel scared and uncertain. Discard the news and embark on your positive journey.

- During the 30 day challenge, keep a close eye on your vocabulary and the thoughts that you think. If your thoughts and words don't compliment your new positive lifestyle, change them accordingly.

- Most importantly, from time-to-time check and see how you're feeling. Your feelings are a feedback mechanism to what you are attracting in your life.

- If you feel happy and positive, you have no choice but to attract happy and positive.

- Tune your vibration to positive and form your new positive preferable lifestyle.

On Gratitude

"Let gratitude be the pillow upon which you kneel to say your nightly prayer. And let faith be the bridge you build to overcome evil and welcome good."
– Maya Angelou

- God/Source has given you the gift of 86,400 seconds today. Have you used one to say thank you?
- Gratitude is the tool that connects you to all the good in life.
- When you're grateful, you focus on the highest and when you focus on the highest, you attract the highest.
- When manifesting your dreams, it's important to be thankful in advance, even before you receive it.
- Telling the universe "thank you" is proof that the manifestation is already yours and you have accepted it.

On Believing And Focusing On The Good

"When you are joyful, when you say yes to life and have fun and project positivity all around you, you become a sun in the center of every constellation, and people want to be near you."
– Shannon L. Alder

- Believe in the good things in life, too many people believe in the opposite.

- The 7:00 o'clock news will constantly shove negative press down your throat, trying to get you to believe the world is a horrible place. They'll tell you about 20% of what's going on in the world, and that 20% is the negative. The other 80% are positive and wonderful news that can raise your vibration. Avoid the news and believe this is positive world. Your belief will prove that you`re right.

- Train your mind to start believing in the good in all

things. Look for the positive in all people and outcomes. You have to vigorously impress the subconscious

- Sooner or later you will develop the belief that the world is a warm, kind place.

- Your belief in the positive outcome will determine how much good you'll experience in the world around you.

- We limit ourselves by the failures of other people, and by the societies' standards.

- We have to remember that we are co-creating the reality that we partake in.

- Whatever you believe, you make true: There is no such thing as a false belief.

- Do you know why all religions think that they are all right, and how all have some proof or form of evidence to what they are saying? It's because their belief makes it so.

- Belief is the most powerful thing in the universe. It's similar to the placebo effect, whatever you truly believe, you eventually make true.

On the Power of Suggestion

"Your mind is working on your future based on a suggestion. The question is on whose suggestion it's working on: Yours or others?"
– Assegid Habtewold

- The power of suggestion is probably the most underrated way to impress the subconscious mind and form new beliefs.

- When you use words and phrases over and over again during a long period of time, you form new belief patterns in the subconscious mind.

- When your subconscious mind starts to believe what is being said, magic happens and you start to manifest your goals much faster.

- Thus, repetition is the key to manifesting what you desire.

- Hold on to your vision and intention with fire and desire.

- Say it to yourself 10x's a day; drill it into the subconscious mind. Miracles will follow shortly.

On Visualization

"We all possess more power and greater possibilities than we realize, and visualizing is one of the greatest of these powers".
– Genevieve Berhrend

- Visualization is such a powerful tool of creation that many philosophers and Quantum Physicists believe it produces creation itself.

- When you imagine a situation in your mind, the subconscious can't tell the difference between what's real or what's imaginary.

- During visualization, your body will react the same way and perform the same acts as if the event was really happening.

- If you keep imagining the same scenario over and over, that impression becomes a belief.
- Your belief sculpts the world around you, it determines the success or failure you experience in life.
- Like my role model Jesus once said, "All things are possible to him who believes."
- If you truly believe in something, nothing will be withheld from you, neither negative nor positive.

On Taking Risks

"Better to live 30 years for of adventure, than a hundred years safe in the corner"
– Jim Rohn

- Those who never jump will never fly. Take risks.
- One thing about this life is, if you don't take any risks, you'll end up staying exactly where you are.
- The essence of life is growth and expansion.
- You can't grow and expand if you're stationary in a corner.
- You have to get out, and take risks and take chances.
- Life should be a never ceasing adventure.

- One of life's greatest secrets is: behind every wall of fear is the reward of receiving everything you always wanted.

- Florence Scovel Shinn says, "The only enemy of man is doubt and fear." Those two things are the only things that can hinder you from achieving your goals and life's purpose.

- Here's the kicker, fear and doubt don't exist. Doubt is a derivative of fear and fear is putting your energy and focus on something that hasn't even happened.

- Fear is False-Evidence-Appearing-Real.

- Fear is a liar and a deceiver. Fear will keep you away from the life you've always envisioned.

- Run through fear and collect the life experiences you came here for.

On Becoming Conscious of the Universal Laws

"To create power is like a magnet, this is true because this creative power operates like a magnet. Give it a strong clear picture of what you want and this creative power starts to work magnetizing conditions about you / attracting to you things, resources, opportunities, circumstances and even the people you need, to help bring to pass in your outer life what you have pictured."

– Claude Bristol

- When you become conscious of the laws that govern our lives, the thoughts, words, feelings, and actions that you have put out, come back to you much more quickly than those who are unaware of these laws.

- For example, one day my wife was poking fun of a picture someone had taken of me. It was a pretty bad picture (bad angle lol) and she got a delight laughing at my slight misfortune. Well, 8 hours later, my wife went on Instagram to browse at her pictures, when to my wife's surprise, her beautician uploaded a less than flattering picture of my wife in the beauty shop. I couldn't help but to chuckle to myself and say, "You reap what you sow".

- Reaping and Sowing is always taking place; it evolves and encompasses everything.
- Many people believe the phrase "you reap what you sow" only applies to the action to take, but that's only half the story. Reaping and Sowing applies to every aspect of your life and it is always returning what you have given.
- If your thoughts are of love and abundance, then that is what you'll reap.
- If your words are of shame and disappointment, then that is what you'll experience.
- If you take actions on prosperity, then prosperity will be the result.
- If your feelings are on "not enough", no matter how much you get, there will simply be not enough. It's so simple, yet few understand it.

On Needing Heroes

"All heroes are shadows of Christ"
– John Piper

- We all need heroes: Heroes give us a blueprint of what's actually possible and what heights we can one day accomplish or surpass.

- I'm not a religious man, but one of my role models so happens to be a carpenter from Galilee, yes, you guessed it, Jesus. My personal research and spiritual findings of Jesus have led me to believe that He was fully aware of these universal laws and has successfully mastered them, thus being able to manipulate the physical world.

- We all have the same ability as Jesus to control matter and to command, "Those things that are not, as though they were".

- I put aside religious dogmas and tap into the person Jesus/Yeshua actually was and his ability to love those who didn't love him.

- Jesus was able to raise hisvibration so high that he was able to control matter and the elements within. The only way to lift your vibration is through love. Love is the strongest unseen force in the universe.

On Deserving Goodness

"We cannot achieve more in life than what we believe in our heart of hearts we deserve to have."
– James R. Ball

- Know that you deserve all the good the universe has for you.
- You will never produce all the good the universe has to offer if you constantly feel as if you don't deserve it.
- The truth is, you are more than deserving.
- Everything you see is a part of God so that means YOU are a part of God.
- Don't you think God deserves the best that life has to offer?

- When you think of the Creator of the universe, do you envision a weak, undeserving, impoverished being, or a being that creates indescribable beauty and the loveliest of thing?
- You are a part of God, and it's your responsibility and birthright to call forth the things you desire during your life experience.

On Training Your Subconscious Mind

"Our subconscious minds have no sense of humor, play no jokes and cannot tell the difference between reality and an imagined thought or image. What we continually think about eventually will manifest in our lives."

– Robert Collier

- Train your subconscious mind while you sleep.

- The subconscious mind does not turn off and does not know how to reject any thoughts or commands you give it.

- If you claim "I'm not good at... ", your subconscious mind takes that statement as truth and will keep sending you examples of "Not being good at ..."

- You have to re-train the subconscious mind and confirm new demands. The best way of doing that is through repetition.

- Every night while I sleep, I play affirmations (on repeat) low enough for me to hear them.
- The subconscious mind picks up those commands and they get embedded in my everyday life. This truly works. We have a plethora of affirmations you can download for free at YouAreCreators.org.

On Breaking the Chains of Conformity

"To be yourself in a world that is constantly trying to make you something else is the greatest accomplishment."
– Ralph Waldo Emerson

- Society teaches us not to stand out. When we conform, we are controlled better.

- Growing up, we are forced to sit in a line, wear school uniforms, and follow the path of "the good student".

- We must break the chains of conformity and become the innovators we were created to be.

- We weren't created to be controlled or to be drones and carbon copies. We were created to be different expressions of "Source".

- We are creators, as we literally create the world around us on a second-by-second basis. This is what "They" don't want you to know.

On Knowledge and Fear

"The cave you most fear to enter contains the greatest treasure."
– Joseph Campbell

- The more you know, the less you fear.
- When I first started to understand the universal laws and how they impacted our lives, that's when I stopped fearing life.
- Life was no longer a mystery to me filled with random events. I understood how things occurred in my life. I could keep them from recurring or discard them altogether.
- When you realize that life yields to your beliefs, and that you can call forth everything you desire, fear will be almost obsolete.

- Knowledge has a funny way of bullying fear and enlightening any situation.
- When you understand the nature of a situation, you can predict the outcome before it happens.
- (Fear or Love)

On "Keep Going" When Things are Bad

"Life was never meant to be a struggle, just a gentle progression from one point to another, much like walking through a valley on a sunny day."
– Stuart Wilde

- If you are going through hell, keep going.
- I was working at a job that I absolutely disliked (and dislike is an understatement). I felt as if I was in a prison, and the only way for me to escape was through my imagination. So during every break, I would pull out a sheet of paper and write how I wanted my life to be. I wrote in the present tense and I acted it out in my mind. I did this so much, the scenarios felt more real than the outside world. To make a long story short; I attracted EVERYTHING I constantly and persistently held in my mind. It wasn't overnight, but it manifested exactly the way it needed to and when it was needed.

- Focus on your desired situation and outcome. Act as if you are already there.
- Speak words that pertains to your desired situation.
- Do the things you would be doing as if your desire was already manifested.
- You are never stuck and change is always constant.
- Focus on the absolute best that can happen.
- If you're going through hell, keep going, this trial is almost over.
- One of my favorite affirmations which was suggested by Louise Hay is, "All is well, out of this situation only good will come and I am safe.

On How Life Responds to You

"What we are today comes from our thoughts of yesterday, and our present thoughts build our life of tomorrow: Our life is the creation of our mind."

– Buddha

- Raise your frequency/mood/attitude and the world will raise with it.

- One of the fantastic discoveries in life is that life responds to the way you feel.

- If you feel happy and excited about the day, life will keep bringing you things that will make you happy and excited.

- Ever notice when you start your day off with a negative attitude, your whole days seem to snowball in a series of negative events?

- The same holds true when you start your day off right; it seems everything goes your way.

- This is beautiful because it gives you the option to

choose what you want to experience.

- Whenever I'm in a bad mood, I realize that I must change it quickly because something is going to manifest from those feelings.

- I've found just by speaking positive words and choosing positive thoughts, I raise my vibration.

- Sometimes singing my favorite song or dancing will lift my mood.

- Remember, when you feel good, you are attracting good things into your life. The key is to feel good most of the time.

- You'll be so used to feeling good that when your feelings take a dive, your subconscious mind will remind you instantly to change your mood into a positive one.

- If you're happy, your world will be happy too.

- Everything responds to your vibration: When you feel stressed, the world will bring you more stress.

- When you're in love, you'll find love everywhere you turn.

- Life is basically a mirror, reflecting back to you the emotions you perpetually put out.
- I know a man who was going through a broken marriage and had a hard time coping with it. He stated that he felt so broken that his "broken" energy affected the things in his home. He said all of a sudden, the microwave handle broke and the oven handle broke. He even stated that some of the door handles broke. That energy of "broken" was so powerful, that physical objects were no match and had to subdue to the command of his feelings.
- I advise you to fill your home with love, and notice the miracles that the vibration of love brings.

On Expectations

"We usually get what we anticipate."
– Claude Bristol

- In every situation, I want you to ask yourself, what's the best that can happen?
- Life has a funny way of abiding to our expectations.
- If we believe life is hard and full of problems, that's exactly what we get.
- But if we believe life is full of wonderful surprises, we'll get that as well.
- When a problematic situation arises, I want you to sit back and think, "What's the absolute best possible outcome?" Then dwell on that.
- Force yourself through the fear, and stay concentrated on your ultimate desired outcome.

On the Law of Attraction

"Each moment of our life, we either invoke or destroy our dreams. We call upon it to become a fact, or we cancel our previous instructions."

– Stuart Wilde

- Test the Law of Attraction for yourself.
- After I learned about the Law of Attraction, I wanted to test it out for myself to see if it really worked. I set the intention to manifest something so random and strange that if I saw this object, it would have to be the Law of Attraction. I wanted to attract a blue apple. So for about 5 days, I would visualize seeing and holding a blue apple. I felt the weight of it in my hand, I saw how lights glared off of it; I made it as real as possible. I did this for about 60 seconds a day, and totally forgot about it after the 5th day. A month passed and I was at a store with my wife and children and suddenly bumped into a shelf. When I turned around to observe what I ran into,

I could not believe my eyes! It was a shelf full of blue apples! Yes, blue apples! It shocked me so much that I was briefly paralyzed for a moment. I have no idea what the blue apples were used for, maybe decoration, but that doesn't matter. I manifested my small desire.

- Small wins give you the extra energy to manifest even larger things.
- Write down your deliberate manifestations and keep tabs on all your victories.
- This is a wonderful tool to remind you how powerful your intentions truly are.
- If you did it once, you can do it again!

On Over-thinking

"All I have seen teaches me to trust the creator of all I have
not seen"
– Ralph Waldo Emerson

- Over-thinking kills your happiness: Life wasn't meant to be a perpetual struggle. Life was meant to be a simple transition from one creation to the next.

- The majority of people over-think the process, thus creating hardship and confusion.

- Life is simple; you get back what you put out, negative or positive.

- When manifesting a new idea, your thoughts should be free-flowing not forced.

- Let the universe give you the next step, instead of you biting your nails and forcefully going out and manually creating something. That won't work.

- All the great men in history have been GIVEN their ideas while in a relaxed state of mind, oftentimes when they were just waking up or in a meditative state-like trance.

- Infinite intelligence works with no struggle involved;the struggle isn't necessary.
- It seems in the mental world, the harder we don't try, the quicker things are done for us.
- Over-thinking can cause stress and anxiety and often leads to very little or nothing getting accomplished.
- The manifestation process was meant to be joyful and exciting.
- Over-thinking is telling the universe that you don't trust the creative process, when in all actuality, the universe produces the manifestations.

- This may sound bad, but try to develop the "I don't care, all is well" attitude.
- When facing a dilemma or problem, have faith and a positive expectancy that everything is being worked out behind closed doors.
- Let it go and trust the Creator of the universe.
- God is always behind the scenes, pulling the strings even if you don't fully see it or understand it.

How The Universe Orchestrates Your Dreams

"You can't connect the dots looking forward; you can only connect them looking backwards. So you have to trust that the dots will somehow connect in your future. You have to trust in something – your gut, destiny, life, karma, whatever. This approach has never let me down, and it has made all the difference in my life."

– Steve Jobs

- You don't have to know how you're going to manifest your desires; that's the universe's job to orchestrate.

- The universe decides how and when you manifest your desires.

- This brings me back to when my wife and I manifested our first house in the most miraculous way... We finally decided that we wanted to move into a house after living in a small 2 bedroom, 1 bathroom apartment with 3 kids. We intended to find a townhouse or a small

starter home. So we wrote out on our goal list that…
"We have a 4 bedroom, 3 bath house with a backyard,
fireplace, and Jacuzzi". We found a townhouse that was
for sale at a reasonable price, but it did not meet our
criteria and was not what we truly wanted. It was a bit
of a fixer upper and had a few dings and scrapes, but
we decided to give it a go. So we decided to attract that
house and give it our full attention. After 2 months of
visualizing, preparing, and negotiating, we discovered
that a couple of missed payments of our student loans
brought our credit score way down. And on top of that,
someone bought the townhouse. We were heartbroken
because we thought that this was our house. But
something told me to look at my goals and remind
myself that I wanted something way bigger and nicer.
So we went on the hunt for another house and found
one in the part of the town we wanted, that met ALL of
our expectations.

So my wife and I held hands and agreed, somehow, someway that this was our house! We went to the store and bought rugs for the front door, small ornaments for decoration, and even started to pack boxes. We were preparing to move into that house even before we spoke with our real estate agent. After speaking with the owners (who are millionaires), and after numerous negotiating, we were approved for our dream house! The house is better than we expected and it exceeded all of our wants and desires.

- The universe loves each and every one of us, and will provide at the perfect time, if we trust and allow.
- But you have to be clear on what you want!

The Universal Laws Are Neutral

"The universe has no restrictions. You place restrictions on the universe with your expectations."

– Deepak Chopra

- The universal laws are neutral: People don't understand how the rich get richer and the poor get poorer. They don't understand that everything is fixated on a set of universal laws that governs all things.

- As Neal Donald Walsch puts it, "The universe only knows "Yes", it has a very limited vocabulary". If you calm "I-am broke", the universe will agree with that statement and will keep bringing you situations that will keep you broke.

- If you claim, "I am prosperous", the universe will support that belief bringing you situations to obtain prosperity.

- These laws don't care if you're black or white, rich or poor, Christian or Muslim.
- They work every time for every person.
- This might sound harsh, but the poor keep getting poorer because of their perpetual thinking patterns and poor actions.
- The rich seem to become even richer because of their belief that money comes easy, and since they have that belief, it does.
- The evidence shows up all around them.
- People get upset with God, blaming God for them being poor and amassing large debt, when God has given us the power and dominion to create anything we want.
- The universal laws are neutral. It doesn't matter if you have $2 or $200,000,000, the law gives you precisely what you put out, poverty or prosperity. My advice is, choose prosperity. Life is better that way.

On Complaining About Your Problems

"Complains are like the clouds that give no rain no matter how thick they gather."
– Israelmore Ayivor

- People who complain about their problems always have them.
- Have you ever known people who constantly complain about their situation and every time you see them, they seem to be getting worse? Well, that is because they're unknowingly perpetuating the misfortune in their life, by simply focusing on it.
- Remember, whatever you give your focus and energy to, negative or positive is growing in your life.
- If you are constantly complaining about what you don't have, you will never have it, and you will produce even more things to complain about.

- If you are in a situation that is less than desirable, you need to use your imagination and visualize your perfect outcome.
- Live into that outcome as if it were already real while including the feelings of the captured moments you see in your head.
- Act as life, and if you hold that state of mind and vibrational frequency, the world will follow suit.
- You must hold onto the vision.

On the Law of Polarity

"There is both joy and suffering on planet Earth because this beautiful world is a world of duality - a world of opposites. There is an opposite side to everything."

– Rhonda Byrne

- The Law of Polarity: This law states that in order for something to exist on this earth, there has to be an opposite.

- If there was no "bad" there could not be "good"; if there was not "cold", there could not be "hot". Everything has its balance and counter opposite.

- You can apply this to your life to help steer you in your desired direction.

- If you're currently in a low point in your life, know that in order for that low point to exist, there has to be its opposite.

- The joy you already seek is out there, and the more you focus on that good, the more it will make its presence known.

On the Power of Concentrated Thoughts

"There's no need for plan B because it distracts from plan A"
– Will Smith

- There's an old Russian proverb that says, "If you chase after two rabbits, you won't catch either one." That's basically saying, if you stretch yourself too thin by trying to do too much, you get nothing accomplished.
- There's power in concentrated thoughts.
- By focusing all of your attention and energy into one thing, your intention acts as a laser beam, harnessing all your creative forces into one direction.
- By manifesting one thing at a time, you will build the faith to manifest even larger things.

On Strengthening Your Faith to Attract Bigger Things

"It's our duty as men and women to proceed as though the limits to our abilities do not exist. We are collaborators in creation... the future of the earth is in our hands."

– Pierre Teilhard de Chardin

- There are levels to this: When people first learn that they create their reality, they set out to manifest something huge and outstanding. That is good and well in a sense, but for most people, manifesting something large will seem unbelievable on a subconscious level.

- Sometimes when trying to manifest large goals, we don't actually believe that we can, so it doesn't materialize. I would recommend manifesting small things, just to strengthen your faith.

- Once you build enough small wins, your faith is now increased to attract even bigger things.

In Conclusion

I hope you enjoyed this book as much as I enjoyed writing it. These are the lessons that have brought me prosperity, good health, and ultimate happiness. Let this knowledge permeate the core of your being, giving you new understandings of the world around you. I love you, God loves you, this is Justin from YouAreCreators, and we support your dreams!